*Subway Psalms:
Finding Faith In
The City*

Contents

FAITH	4
WINDS OF CHANGE	4
RESCUED BY LOVE	6
PRICELESS OFFERING	7
A PSALM OF PRAISE	8
THE VOICE OF LOVE	9
A PATHWAY TO REDEMPTION	10
THE WHISPER OF GRACE	11
THE DANCE OF GRACE	13
THE GIFT OF GRACE	14
DELIVERANCE	16
THE SONG	17
THE WEIGHT	18
THE FLOOD	19
LADDER	20
THE HOPE BEHIND THE SHADOW	22
REDEMPTION	24
HEARKEN	26
WEAKNESS	28
ROAD	29
STORMS	30
HEARTS	31
FIRE & WATER	32

THE UNION	*33*
IN HIS	*34*
AFRAID	*35*
IN HIS LOVE	*36*
SHADOW	*37*
OPEN	*38*
HOLD	*39*
GOSPEL	*40*
THE WORD OF GOD	*41*
A LEAP OF TRUST	*42*
THE UNSEEN BRIDGE	*43*
THE ANCHOR'S EMBRACE	*44*
THE FATIHFUL GARDENER	*45*
GUIDING STAR	*46*
SYMPHONY OF TRUST	*47*
UNFULING FAITH	*48*
MOUNTAIN'S OF SHADOW	*49*
TAPESTRY OF BELIEF	*50*
FAITHFUL RIVER	*51*
UNBREAKABLE THREAD	*52*
LIGHTOUSE OF THE SOUL	*53*
SILENT FAITH	*54*
FAITH'S UNWAVERING EMBRACE	*55*
DANCE OF CONVICTION	*56*
A FOREST OF BELIEF	*57*
VOYAGE	*58*
THE PATH OF TRUST	*59*
FLAME	*60*

ECHO	61
THE JOURNEY	62
THE SOARING FAITH	63
THE QUILT	64
KEY	65
THE STORM	66
A SYMPHONY OF TRUST	67
MOUNTAIN	68
THE HARVEST	69
SHELTER	70
GARDEN OF GRACE	71
TOUCH OF GRACE	72
THE FOUNTAIN	73
THE RIVER	74
SYMPHONY	75
DIVINE AMNESTY	76
COMPASSION	77
THE GIFT	78
MERCY'S DAWN	79
FATHER'S LOVE	80
POWER OF FORGIVENESS	81
JOY OF REDEMPTION	82
GRACE OF GOD	83
HOPE OF FORGIVENESS	84
UNFALLING LOVE OF GOD	85
LIVING WORD	86
VOICE	87
LIGHT OF THE WORD	88

WELLSPRING OF TRUTH	89
THE WORDS EMBRACE	90
THE BREATH	91
PILLARS	92
ETERNITY	93
UNFAILING WORD	94
THE TAPESTRY	95

FAITH

My faith in God is like a steadfast tower,
Guiding me through life's darkest hour.
It brings me hope, it brings me peace,
A comfort that will never cease.

In God I trust, in all my ways,
Through all my trials, He always stays.
His love and mercy, they never fade,
My faith in Him, it will not sway.

My heart sings praises to His holy name,
For all the blessings that He has claimed.
He is my rock, my strength, my shield,
In Him I find my joy and yield.

So, I will walk by faith, not by sight,
With confidence in God's guiding light.
My faith in Him, it will not waver,
For in His love, I will always find my anchor.

WINDS OF CHANGE

Blowing softly, yet so strong within.

It guides us, it comforts, it leads the way,

Bringing peace and joy to us each day.

It whispers to our hearts, it speaks truth,

And gives us strength, to stand our ground, forsooth.

It fills us with love, and sets us free,

From the worries of this world, and the troubles we see. With God by my side, I have no fear,

His love and protection, always near.

He is my strength, my rock, my shield,

In Him, I find the peace I need.

No storm can shake me, no trial defeat,

For God's love is greater, can't be beat.

He holds my hand, guides me through,

With Him, I know I'll make it through.

No matter what comes my way,

With God by my side, I'll stand tall and say,

I have no fear, for He's always near,

And His love and grace, they wipe away my tear.

So, I'll walk with courage, and not look back,

With faith in God, I'll stay on track.

For with Him by my side, I have no fear,

And His love and protection, always near. The spirit of God, it is like the wind,

The spirit of God, it is like fire,

Burning bright, with a holy desire.

It ignites our hearts, and lights our way,

And shows us the path, to walk in His way.

So let us open our hearts, to the spirit of God,

And allow it to fill us and lead us on.

For with the spirit of God, we are never alone, And His love and guidance, will always be shown.

RESCUED BY LOVE

Salvation through Christ, it is a gift so rare,

A treasure beyond measure, beyond compare.

It brings us peace, it brings us hope,

And wipes away all our sins, with a gentle rope.

It sets us free, from the chains of sin,

And gives us a new life, to begin.

It restores us, to the image of God,

And gives us a future, that's bright and broad.

Through faith in Christ, we are saved,

And receive the gift of eternal life, unshaved.

We are reconciled, to our heavenly Father,

And become part of His family, forever and after.

So let us rejoice, and give thanks to God,

For the gift of salvation, through His son, the Lord.

For it is by grace, that we are saved,

And through faith in Christ, we are forever redeemed and brave.

PRICESLESS OFFERING

The love of God for man is vast and true,

It reaches far beyond what eyes can view.

It shines like stars and flows like a river,

Bringing peace, hope, and joy forever.

It's patient, kind, and never fails or fades,

It lifts us up when we've fallen from grace.

It sees beyond our flaws and mistakes,

And wraps us in its warm and tender embrace.

It suffered pain and died on Calvary,

So, we could live with Him eternally.

It paid the price for all our sins,

So, we could be free from condemnation's chains.

This love of God for man is pure and bright,

It shines in darkness and dispels the night.

It gives us hope and helps us to survive,

And fills our hearts with love that will abide.

A PSALM OF PRAISE

A song of joy in God's ways.

It tells of one who fears the Lord,

Whose heart is filled with love outpoured.

Their deeds are just, their heart is pure,

Their trust in God will always endure.

Their children will be blessed, it's said,

Their wealth and name will never fade.

They give to those in need with grace,

Their light shines bright in every place.

Their hearts are firm, their spirit strong,

Their righteousness will never do wrong.

They'll never be afraid, it's clear,

For God will always be near.

Their heart will be at peace, it's said,

For they have put their trust in God instead.

So let us sing this psalm with glee,

And live our lives in humility.

For those who fear the Lord, it's true,

Will be blessed with peace and joy anew.

THE VOICE OF LOVE

Sin creeps in like a shadow, dark and sly,

It whispers lies and leads us from the light.

It takes us down a path we shouldn't tread,

And leaves us feeling lost and filled with dread.

But in our hearts, a voice is calling out,

Urging us to turn and cast our sin about.

It's the voice of love, the voice of grace,

Inviting us to seek a better place.

So, we must listen, and we must obey,

And turn from sin and choose a better way.

We must confess, and seek forgiveness too,

And trust in God to make us pure and true.

For in repentance, we find release,

From the weight of sin, and the guilt and peace.

We find a love that's greater than our fall,

And a grace that will lift us when we call.

So let us turn from sin and seek the Lord,

And trust in His love to heal and restore.

For in repentance, we find new birth,

And a life of joy and peace on this earth.

A PATHWAY TO REDEMPTION

Deliverance, a word of hope,

A promise of a brighter slope.

A way out of the pain and strife,

A release from the chains of life.

It comes like a ray of light,

Breaking through the dark of night.

A guiding hand to lead the way,

A lighthouse shining bright each day.

It brings us peace and comfort too,

And lifts us up when we are feeling blue.

It gives us strength to face our fears,

And wipes away our endless tears.

It frees us from our doubts and pain,

And helps us rise above the strain.

It shows us love can conquer all,

And helps us stand when we might fall.

So let us trust in this great power,

And let it lead us in this hour.

For deliverance is here for us,

A gift from God, a grace so just.

THE WHISPER OF GRACE

Upon the winds of morning's tender light,

A gentle force, a whisper soft and sweet,

Descends upon the chaos of the night,

And brings the taste of harmony complete.

In quiet moments, grace reveals her face,

A subtle kiss of hope upon the breeze,

Transforming pain, despair and dire straits,

Into a sacred dance, a life at ease.

For grace is ever-present, always near,

A quiet strength that seeks to mend and heal,

To lift the heart, and vanquish doubt and fear,

And in the darkest hour, its truth reveal.

So, listen close, and let grace be your guide,

In love and peace, with open arms, reside.

A Glimpse of Grace

The sun's warm rays awaken slumbering earth,

And grace, a golden thread, weaves life anew,

In every breath, each sigh of love and mirth,

It finds a home, a place to rest and imbue.

A fleeting glimpse, an echo in the wind,

Yet potent as the sun that lights the day,

A force unseen that binds and drives all things,

And in its subtle touch, the truth conveys.

The strength of grace can move the hardest heart,

And bend the stiffest will to mercy's sway,

In moments, life's most bitter wounds can part,

As love and understanding hold their way.

Embrace the glimpse of grace that lingers near,

And let its tender touch dispel your fears.

THE DANCE OF GRACE

With every step, the dancers glide and sway,

In harmony, they share a love unseen,

The music of the spheres, the breath of day,

A wondrous dance of grace, a world serene.

A pas de deux, the heart and soul entwined,

In tender, sweet communion, they become,

A perfect fusion, body, spirit, mind,

An ode to life, and love's eternal drum.

This dance of grace, a moment's gentle touch,

A symphony that plays within the soul,

In silent spaces, whispers soft and hushed,

And leads us to a place of peace untold.

So let the dance of grace within you grow,

In every step, let love and kindness show.

THE GIFT OF GRACE

The gift of grace, like rain upon the soil,

Quenches the thirst of hearts that long for peace,

A solace in the midst of strife and toil,

A balm to heal the wounds that never cease.

In quiet moments, grace unfolds its wings,

And wraps the world in tender, loving care,

A touch of light, a joy that softly sings,

And lifts the weary soul from dark despair.

To see the gift of grace, we must be still,

And listen for the whispers in the air,

For in the silence, truth is there revealed,

And grace will find us, ready, and prepared.

Receive the gift of grace, and let it shine,

Within your heart, a beacon, pure and divine.

The Heart of Grace

A heart of grace beats gently in the chest,

A steady pulse of love and compassion,

A fire that burns within, and gives us rest,

A source of strength in times of tribulation.

In every smile, and every tear that's shed,

The heart of grace reveals its gentle face,

A guiding light that leads through fear and dread,

And brings us home, to love's eternal grace.

To find the heart of grace, look deep within,

And see the light that shines in every soul,

For there, amidst the darkness and the din,

A spark of love, a whisper soft and whole.

Unveil the heart of grace that dwells inside,

And let it guide you, ever by your side.

DELIVERANCE

Deliverance, a word of hope,

A promise of a brighter slope.

A way out of the pain and strife,

A release from the chains of life.

It comes like a ray of light,

Breaking through the dark of night.

A guiding hand to lead the way,

A lighthouse shining bright each day.

It brings us peace and comfort too,

And lifts us up when we are feeling blue.

It gives us strength to face our fears,

And wipes away our endless tears.

It frees us from our doubts and pain,

And helps us rise above the strain.

It shows us love can conquer all,

And helps us stand when we might fall.

So let us trust in this great power,

And let it lead us in this hour.

For deliverance is here for us,

A gift from God, a grace so just.

THE SONG

The Song of Solomon, a book of love,

A tale of two hearts intertwined as one.

It speaks of passion, pure and true,

And of a love that's greater than the sun.

It speaks of longing, and of yearning,

Of sweet whispers in the dead of night.

It speaks of beauty, and of learning,

And of the joy that love can bring to light.

It speaks of trust, and of devotion,

Of two hearts beating as one, it's said.

It speaks of grace, and of emotion,

And of the love that's alive and well in bed.

It's a song of hope, a song of peace,

A hymn of love that will never cease.

It's a reminder of the power of love,

And of the blessings that come from above.

THE WEIGHT

Anxiety, a weight so heavy,

A burden that's hard to bear.

It creeps in like a thief, unsavory,

And steals our peace and joy with care.

It grips our hearts and clouds our minds,

And makes us doubt and fear the worst.

It keeps us up at night, confined,

And leaves us feeling broken, cursed.

But in the midst of all this pain,

There's a help that's always near.

A God who loves and will sustain,

And wipe away our every tear.

He's a rock that's firm and strong,

A shelter in the stormy weather.

He's a light that shines so long,

And leads us to a place of better.

So, when anxiety creeps in,

And you feel like you can't go on,

Just call on God, and you will win,

For He will lift you up and carry on.

THE FLOOD

The flood came like a rushing tide,

A storm of water, dark and wide.

It covered all the earth below,

And washed away the seeds of woe.

The rains fell hard, the winds did blow,

And all the creatures, great and small,

Were swept away, their lives below,

In the deluge, that did fall.

But in the midst of all the rain,

A ray of hope did shine and gleam.

For Noah, in his faith and trust,

Was saved, and given a new start, a just.

And from the ark, he saw a sign,

A rainbow, stretching wide and bright.

A symbol of the Lord's good word,

And of the promise, that was heard.

So let us find new life in Christ,

And rise above the storm and strife.

For in His love, we'll always find,

The hope and grace, of a new life.

LADDER

The ladder of life, it rises high,
A path that leads us to the sky.

It winds and twists, it climbs and falls,

And tests our strength, and answers calls.

We struggle up, with weary feet,

And feel the weight of life's defeat.

We reach for handholds, one by one,

And hope to make it to the top, begun.

But sometimes, we lose our grip,

And fall, with nothing to hold on to.

We feel alone, and in a slip,

And wonder if we'll make it through.

But in that moment, when we pray,

And reach out for a helping hand,

The grace of God comes our way,

And lifts us up, to stand.

For He is there, with open arms,

Ready to catch us, and to hold.

His grace is strong, it has no harm,

And it will never let us go, bold.

So let us trust in His good grace,

And climb the ladder of life with peace.

For in His love, we'll always find,

The strength to rise and climb with grace.

THE HOPE BEHOND THE SHADOW

Sin, a shadow that creeps in,
A darkness that clouds the light.

It takes us down a path within,

And leads us to a deathless night.

It's a weight that pulls us low,

A burden that's hard to bear.

It steals our joy, and peace, and glow,

And leaves us feeling lost and scared.

Death, a door that opens wide,

A threshold that we all must cross.

It takes us from this world aside,

And leaves us with a heavy loss.

But in the midst of all this pain,

There's a hope that's always near.

A love that will sustain,

And wipe away our every tear.

For Jesus died to take our place,

And pay the price for our own sin.

He rose again, with grace,

And conquered death and rose again.

So let us trust in His great love,

And find in Him, our peace and rest.

For in His love, we'll rise above,

The shadow of sin, and death's request.

REDEMPTION

Redemption, his mission, to free us from sin,

And lead us to glory, forever to win.

From ancient of days, this promise was made,

By prophets and seers, who foretold his crusade.

A messiah, they said, would come to redeem,

A lamb to be slain, so that we may gleam.

And lo, he came, born in a manger so low,

To humble beginnings, his life here did show.

A teacher, a healer, a friend to the lost,

His love was unending, no matter the cost.

He walked on the water, and calmed the storm's might,

Fed the hungry and gave the blind their sight.

Healing the sick, and raising the dead,

His power and grace, his followers led.

But his ultimate task, on Calvary's hill,

Was to suffer and die, as was his Father's will.

A sacrifice made, to atone for our sins,

To bring us redemption, and new life begins.

Through his blood, our ransom was paid,

And from death's sting, we are forever stayed.

Redemption, our song, to the lamb on the throne,

Our savior, our king, forever to own.

So let us sing, and lift up our voice,

To the one who redeemed us, let us rejoice.

For by his grace, we are saved and set free,

Forever his children, for all eternity.

HEARKEN

Hearken, ye people, and hark to my tale,

Of a savior who hath come to prevail.

Redemption, his mission, to free us from sin,

And lead us to glory, forever to win.

From ancient of days, this promise was made,

By prophets and seers, who foretold his crusade.

A messiah, they said, would come to redeem,

A lamb to be slain, so that we may gleam.

And lo, he came, born in a manger so low,

To humble beginnings, his life here did show.

A teacher, a healer, a friend to the lost,

His love was unending, no matter the cost.

He walked on the water, and calmed the storm's might,

Fed the hungry and gave the blind their sight.

Healing the sick, and raising the dead,

His power and grace, his followers led.

But his ultimate task, on Calvary's hill,

Was to suffer and die, as was his Father's will.

A sacrifice made, to atone for our sins,

To bring us redemption, and new life begins.

Through his blood, our ransom was paid,

And from death's sting, we are forever stayed.

Redemption, our song, to the lamb on the throne,

Our savior, our king, forever to own.

So let us sing, and lift up our voice,

To the one who redeemed us, let us rejoice.

For by his grace, we are saved and set free,

Forever his children, for all eternity.

WEAKENESS

Pain sears my soul like a sharpened sword,

A burden heavy, a cross to bear.

In trials and tribulations, I'm floored,

Lost and broken, drowning in despair.

But in my weakness, I call upon His name,

And find strength in the One who bore our sin.

For Christ endured the cross and the shame,

And in His resurrection, we find life again.

So, though I suffer, I know it's not in vain,

For through my pain, He brings forth joy and gain.

ROAD

he road I walk is filled with thorns,

And every step brings piercing pain.

The weight of sorrow makes me mourn,

As I struggle through life's endless rain.

But in the darkness, I find a light,

A hope that burns with steady flame.

For in His mercy, God gives sight,

And with His love, He bears my shame.

So, though the road may be long and rough,

I know He's with me every step.

For in His grace, I've found enough,

To endure and overcome my deepest depths.

STORMS

Through the storm of suffering and pain,

I cry out to the Lord above,

And find peace in His holy name.

The darkness may try to take its claim,

And the road may be rough and tough,

But through the storm of suffering and pain,

I cling to the promise that He came,

To heal and save and lift us up,

And find peace in His holy name.

For He bore our sins and our shame,

And in His love, we find enough,

Through the storm of suffering and pain.

So, I'll endure with faith and aim,

And trust in His grace and His love,

And find peace in His holy name,

Through the storm of suffering and pain.

HEARTS

Two hearts, entwined by God's divine hand,

Joined in marriage, through thick and thin.

Through trials and tests, they take a stand,

And commit to love until life's end.

For love is patient, love is kind,

And true love never fades away.

In Christ, their love will always bind,

And through His grace, they'll never stray.

So may their love be a shining light,

A testament to God's great plan.

For in their love, we see God's might,

And in their faith, we see His hand.

FIRE & WATER

Love was the flame that brought them together,

A bond that nothing could ever sever.

With hearts full of hope and eyes full of light,

They vowed to love and to hold, through the night.

Their love was like a river, flowing deep and wide,

A love that never falters, a love that never dies.

In Christ, they found their anchor, their rock,

A love that never fails, a love that never stops.

Through trials and tests, they stood firm,

In Christ, their love was the greatest term.

For in His grace, they found their strength,

And in His love, they found their depth.

So let us honor their love today,

And in their example, let us find our way.

For in Christ, we find our truest love,

And in His grace, we find our home above.

THE UNION

A union blessed by God above,

A vow of love and commitment true.

In Christ, they find their perfect love.

Through every trial and every rough,

They stand together, with hearts renewed.

A union blessed by God above.

For in their love, we see His love,

A love that's faithful, strong, and true.

In Christ, they find their perfect love.

And through His grace, they rise above,

Every trial and every storm they've been through.

A union blessed by God above.

So let us honor their commitment true,

And in their love, let us see God's view.

For in Christ, they find their perfect love,

A union blessed by God above.

IN HIS

In Christ, we find the courage to be bold,

And face our fears with steadfast heart and soul.

For in His love, we find our perfect mold,

And in His grace, our fears are made whole.

So let us not be afraid of the dark,

For in His light, we see the truth revealed.

And let us trust in His holy mark,

For in His blood, our fears are repealed.

For perfect love casts out all fear,

And in His love, we find our strength to stand.

So let us cling to His words so dear,

And in His love, we'll find the Promised Land.

AFRAID

Fear is a thief that steals our peace,

A darkness that can never cease.

But in His light, we find our way,

And in His love, we find our day.

For in His grace, we find our strength,

And in His mercy, our fears are lengthened.

So let us not be afraid to be bold,

For in His love, we'll never grow old.

For perfect love casts out all fear,

And in His love, we'll find our way clear.

So let us trust in His holy name,

And in His love, we'll never be the same.

IN HIS LOVE

In the face of fear and doubt,

We can stand tall and shout.

For in His love, we find our way,

And in His grace, we'll never sway.

For perfect love casts out all fear,

And in His love, we'll find our cheer.

So let us trust in His holy name,

And in His love, we'll never be the same.

For He is our rock, our solid ground,

And in His love, our fears are drowned.

So let us take His hand and be bold,

For in His love, we'll never grow old.

And through the trials and the tests,

We'll stand strong, our faith confessed.

For in His love, we'll never fall,

And in His grace, we'll stand tall.

SHADOW

Fear is a shadow, a fleeting thing,

A darkness that can never last.

With God by our side, we can always sing.

For in His love, we find our wing,

A courage that will never pass.

Fear is a shadow, a fleeting thing.

In Christ, we find our strength to cling,

And through His love, we'll never crash.

With God by our side, we can always sing.

So let us trust in His holy ring,

And in His grace, our fears are surpassed.

Fear is a shadow, a fleeting thing.

For perfect love casts out all fear,

And in His love, we find our steadfast.

With God by our side, we can always sing.

So let us cling to His holy word,

And in His love, our fears are deterred.

Fear is a shadow, a fleeting thing,

With God by our side, we can always sing.

OPEN

The truth of salvation rings out clear,

A gift of grace that we cannot earn.

It is a love that casts out all fear,

And from our sins, we are free to turn.

Repentance is the key to our release,

A turning from the life we lived before.

For in His love, we find our perfect peace,

And in His grace, we find an open door.

So let us turn to Christ with hearts that yearn,

And in His love, we'll find our saving grace.

For in His truth, we'll find the way to learn,

And in His mercy, we'll find a brand new place.

HOLD

Persecution comes to those who speak the truth,

A test of faith that's hard to understand.

For in the world, we find our every proof,

That following Christ is not an easy plan.

But in His love, we find the strength to stand,

And in His grace, we find a way to cope.

For in His mercy, we find a helping hand,

A light that guides us through life's every slope.

So let us hold to Christ with steadfast hope,

And in His truth, we'll find the way to go.

For in His love, we find a strength that's bold,

And in His grace, we'll find the strength to grow.

For in His truth, we find our every light,

And in His love, we find the way of might.

GOSPEL

The Gospel speaks of love and sacrifice, Of how the Word of God became a man, And how he suffered on the cross, our price To pay for sin, and lead us to God's plan.

The Gospel offers hope and grace to all, A way to turn from darkness to the light, To answer God's redeeming, loving call, And follow him forever in his sight.

Oh, Gospel true, your message is so sweet, A balm to heal our souls, to set us free, To help us walk in righteousness and meet Our Savior, who has died for you and me.

Let's share this Gospel with a broken world And see the power of God's love unfurled.

THE WORD OF GOD

The Word of God is living and active, A double-edged sword that cuts so deep, It pierces to the heart, and is reactive To all our thoughts, and secrets we would keep.

The Word of God is true, and always right, A lamp to guide us through life's darkest hour, A compass that will keep us in the light, A source of wisdom, and of saving power.

Oh, Word of God, so holy and divine, Your message is so pure, so full of grace, A fountain of life that will ever shine, And lead us to our Savior's loving face.

Let's treasure God's Word, and let it dwell, Deep in our hearts, where it will ever swell.

A LEAP OF TRUST

In the quiet whispers of the night,

A seed of faith takes root and grows,

With each new breath and beam of light,

The tender tendrils stretch and glow.

In storms and sun, it finds its way,

Its strength unknown, yet ever sure,

A beacon through the darkest day,

A testament that will endure.

THE UNSEEN BRIDGE

Above the chasm, vast and deep,

A bridge unseen, yet firmly laid,

We take our steps in faith, we leap,

And find our fears begin to fade.

For as we walk the hidden path,

Our trust in something greater grows,

We conquer doubt, defy the wrath,

And reach the heights that love bestows.

THE ANCHOR'S EMBRACE

Like anchors firm in oceans deep,

Faith holds us fast through wind and wave,

Its grasp secure, our souls to keep,

When life's fierce tempests try to rave.

And though the night may seem so long,

And waters dark, with dangers rife,

This anchor's hold remains so strong,

A steadfast guide through storms of life.

THE FATIHFUL GARDENER

In fertile soil, the Gardener toils,

With gentle hands and patient heart,

Each seedling nurtured, as it coils,

In faith, a blooming work of art.

Through drought and flood, through sun and shade,

The Gardener's love, unwavering,

In faith, a bountiful cascade,

Of blossoms bright, their fragrance sing.

GUIDING STAR

A distant star, unseen by day,

Yet in the night, it shines so bright,

A beacon true, to guide our way,

And lead us through the deepest night.

With faith, we follow where it leads,

In hope, our steps are firmly set,

And trusting that our hearts will heed,

The guidance of this light, we met.

SYMPHONY OF TRUST

An orchestra of souls and hearts,

In harmony, united stand,

Each part unique, with faith their art,

They blend in concert, grand and grand.

A symphony of trust and love,

Resounding through the vast expanse,

Their melodies, like wings of doves,

Take flight and lift us in their dance.

UNFULING FAITH

Faith, like a bud, in secret grows,

Unfurling slow, its hidden grace,

In time, its beauty is disclosed,

A wonder, that no storm can chase.

And as the petals bloom and spread,

Their fragrance fills the air around,

A testament, in whispers said,

Of faith, unwavering, profound.

MOUNTAIN'S OF SHADOW

In the mountain's shadow, faith abides,

Unyielding as the stones below,

Through time's relentless march and tides,

It stands, a fortress of the soul.

Though winds may howl, and rains may fall,

And lightning strike with fearsome might,

This faith remains, unbroken, tall,

A refuge, in the darkest night.

TAPESTRY OF BELIEF

Intricate threads of faith entwined,

A tapestry of love and trust,

Each strand a color, bold or shy,

A masterpiece, in patience thrust.

And as the weaver's hand designs,

This work of art unfolds, complete,

A testament of faith, that shines,

In every fiber, strong and sweet.

FAITHFUL RIVER

A river, in its ceaseless flow,

Meanders on, through vale and glen,

Its faith in unseen paths below,

A mystery, we can't comprehend.

Yet on it moves, with grace and might,

Through twists and turns, through calm and strife,

A symbol of enduring light

UNBREAKABLE THREAD

A slender thread, so fine and frail,

Yet bound with faith, it cannot break,

Though tempests rage and storms assail,

It holds us fast, for love's own sake.

Invisible, yet ever strong,

This thread of faith, it spans the years,

Connecting hearts, where they belong,

Through joy and sorrow, hope and fears.

LIGHTOUSE OF THE SOUL

Upon a rocky shore, it stands,

A lighthouse, bright and tall and true,

With faith, it guides through shifting sands,

And leads us safely to the blue.

A beacon in the darkest night,

A light that never fades or dims,

This faith, our compass, ever right,

A song of hope, the heart's own hymn.

SILENT FAITH

In whispers soft, or silence deep,

Faith weaves its subtle, quiet thread,

A gentle touch, a promise keep,

A wordless bond, in stillness bred.

And though it speaks no loud acclaim,

This silent faith, it bears us up,

Through darkest night, and stormy gale,

A refuge, in a loving cup.

FAITH'S UNWAVERING EMBRACE

Like arms outstretched, in warm embrace,

Faith holds us close, its love so pure,

In every trial, time and place,

A shelter, ever strong and sure.

And as we cling to faith's embrace,

Our hearts are lifted, hope restored,

For in its touch, we find the grace,

To face the storms and trust the Lord.

DANCE OF CONVICTION

In rhythmic steps, we dance and sway,

Our feet, they follow faith's own beat,

Through night and day, we trust the way,

Our hearts, in unison, repeat.

This dance of faith, a sacred art,

A testament of trust and love,

Each step, a journey of the heart,

To higher realms and heights above.

A FOREST OF BELIEF

A forest dense, with faith as trees,

Their roots entwined, beneath the ground,

A shelter for the weary breeze,

Their branches strong, their trunks unbound.

Each tree, a symbol of the faith,

That binds us all, both near and far,

In unity, we find our strength,

Beneath the canopy of stars.

VOYAGE

Upon a sea, so vast and wide,

A ship sets sail, with faith its guide,

Through storms and waves, it charts its course,

With trust, it finds its truest source.

And as the winds of change blow strong,

This ship of faith sails ever on,

A testament to love and trust,

A voyage, through the endless dusk.

THE PATH OF TRUST

A winding path, through meadows sweet,

And mountains high, with faith as guide,

We place our steps, with trust replete,

In hope, our journey never dies.

For as we walk the path of trust,

Our hearts are filled with love and grace,

The landscape changes, as it must,

Yet faith remains, our rock and base.

FLAME

A single flame, in darkness burns,

Its light, a beacon of pure faith,

Through wind and storm, it never turns,

A constant guide, through life's own maze.

And as we follow where it leads,

Our hearts alight with love and hope,

This faithful flame, it plants the seeds,

Of trust, that helps us all to cope.

ECHO

An echo, soft and pure and clear,

Resounds through valleys, hills, and dales,

A testament of faith so dear,

Its message, like a song, prevails

"Faith's Resilient Blossom"

In arid lands, where rain is rare,

A fragile bloom, through faith, emerges,

Defying drought, with colors fair,

A testament to life's own urges.

Its petals, delicate and bright,

A symbol of enduring trust,

That even in the harshest light,

Faith blooms and turns the dust to lush.

THE JOURNEY

A winding road, through life we tread,

With faith our compass, true and bold,

In every twist and turn we're led,

To revelations yet untold.

We trust the path, and as we roam,

With hearts uplifted, ever strong,

This faithful journey leads us home,

To where we've always known we'd belong.

THE SOARING FAITH

Like eagles soaring high above,

With wings outstretched, we rise on faith,

In thermals strong, on currents of love,

We trust in unseen winds to keep us safe.

And as we climb, to heights unknown,

Our hearts, they sing a song of trust,

For in our flight, we're never alone,

Faith guides us on, it's more than just.

THE QUILT

A quilt of many colors bright,

Each patch a symbol of our faith,

Together sewn, through love and light,

A tapestry of warmth and grace.

And as we wrap ourselves within,

This quilt of trust and faith combined,

We find the strength to rise again,

A testament to hearts entwined.

KEY

A golden key, with faith imbued,

Unlocks the doors to realms unseen,

With trust, we step into the new,

And face the world with hearts serene.

And as we journey, hand in hand,

Our faith, the key to love's own gate,

We find the strength to understand,

That trust in life can never abate.

THE STORM

In tempests fierce, and raging gales,

A storm of faith, it stirs within,

Its power, like the wind, prevails,

A force unyielding, fierce and keen.

And as we face the storm of trust,

Our hearts are molded, shaped anew,

A testament to love and thrust,

A beacon, shining bright and true.

A SYMPHONY OF TRUST

A chorus sweet, of voices raised,

In harmony, they sing of faith,

Their melodies, like sunlit rays,

Illuminate the darkest place.

And as we listen to their song,

Our hearts, they echo trust and love,

A symphony, that carries on,

Through time and space, and realms above.

MOUNTAIN

A fountain, clear and pure and bright,

Its waters, symbols of our faith,

In constant flow, both day and night,

A source of life, that never wanes.

And as we drink from faith's own well,

Our hearts are filled with trust and grace,

A testament to love's own spell,

A fountain, that can ne'er be replaced.

THE HARVEST

In fields of gold, we reap and sow,

The seeds of faith, both small and great,

With patient hands, we tend and grow,

A harvest rich, and ripe with fate.

And as we gather in our yield,

Our hearts are full of love and trust,

A testament to faith's own shield,

A bounty, that can never rust.

SHELTER

A haven safe, from storm and strife,

A shelter built on faith and love,

With trust, we face the trials of life,

And find our refuge from above.

And as we rest within its walls,

Our hearts are soothed, our spirits calmed

GARDEN OF GRACE

In gardens lush with colors bold and bright,

A sanctuary where grace and beauty dwell,

Each petal, leaf, and bloom a wondrous sight,

A testament to life's sweet miracle.

Amidst the verdant green and vibrant hues,

The whispers of the wind, the scent of rain,

A symphony of grace in every view,

A haven from the chaos and the pain.

So, tend the garden of your soul with care,

And cultivate the seeds of love and peace,

For in this sacred space, you'll find repair,

And all your heart's desires shall be released.

The garden of grace, a refuge from the fray,

A balm to soothe the heart and light the way.

TOUCH OF GRACE

A gentle touch, a warmth that knows no bounds,

A soothing balm that calms the storm within,

The touch of grace, a force both strong and sound,

A breath of love that makes the heart begin.

In times of pain, when darkness clouds the mind,

And shadows cast their pall upon the soul,

The touch of grace can lift the veil, unwind,

And guide us to a place of peace untold.

To feel the touch of grace, we must be still,

And open up our hearts to love's embrace,

For there, amidst the quiet, grace will spill,

And fill our lives with light, and endless grace.

So welcome in the touch of grace divine,

And let it heal your heart, and spirit refine.

THE FOUNTAIN

From depths unknown, a wellspring pure and clear,

A fountain of grace, a source of boundless love,

It flows through every heart, and every tear,

A gift bestowed from heaven high above.

The waters of this fountain wash us clean,

And bathe our souls in light and tender care,

A healing force that makes our spirits keen,

A touch of hope that banishes despair.

To drink from this fountain, we must trust,

And open up our hearts to love's sweet call,

For in the end, it's love that's true and just,

And grace, the force that binds and heals us all.

So, seek the fountain of grace, and be restored,

In love's embrace, let your spirit soar.

THE RIVER

A river of grace, it flows through time and space,

Its currents soft and gentle, yet so strong,

A constant presence, nourishing life's embrace,

And carrying us to where we all belong.

In moments of despair, or deepest doubt,

The river of grace will gently guide our way,

A subtle force that moves us in and out,

Of darkness, and into the light of day.

To find the river of grace, we must let go,

And trust in life's great wisdom to unfold,

For in the flow of grace, we come to know,

A love eternal, a truth that's never old.

Embrace the river of grace, and let it guide,

To shores of peace, where love and hope reside.

SYMPHONY

A symphony of grace, a song of love,

That echoes through the chambers of our hearts,

In melodies that soar to skies above,

And weave a tapestry of life's great art.

Each note, a breath of grace that fills our lungs,

And brings us closer to our deepest truth,

A harmony that binds and gently clings,

To every moment, every dream, and youth.

To hear the symphony of grace, be still,

And let the music of the soul resound,

For in its strains, we find the strength and will,

To overcome the trials that abound.

So, listen close, and let the symphony,

Of grace and love, forever set you free.

DIVINE AMNESTY

In mercy, grace, and love divine,

Our sins He bore on Calvary's shrine.

The cross, the pain, the shame, the death,

He gave to give us life and breath.

Forgiveness free, for all who seek,

A pardon pure, a soul that's meek.

His blood atones for every wrong,

And makes us pure, with praise and song.

COMPASSION

The Lord's compassion never ends,

His mercy flows, His grace transcends.

Our sins He buries in the deep,

And washes us with love so deep.

He holds us in His loving hands,

And leads us to His perfect plans.

Our fears, our doubts, He casts away,

And fills us with His peace each day.

THE GIFT

The gift of forgiveness, so sweet and so rare,

Is given to all who confess and who care.

It flows from the heart of our Savior above,

And fills us with peace, with joy, and with love.

It frees us from guilt, from shame, and from pain,

And makes us new, with a heart that's plain.

We're cleansed by the blood that He shed on the tree,

And live forever, with Him, holy and free.

MERCY'S DAWN

At mercy's dawn, the light appears,

And wipes away our guilty tears.

The Son of God, in love, forgives,

And by His grace, forever lives.

His mercy, like a gentle stream,

Flows over us and makes us clean.

Our past, our present, all are gone,

And in His love, we're forever one.

FATHER'S LOVE

The Father's love, so pure and true,

Forgives our sins and makes us new.

His grace, like rain, falls from above,

And fills our hearts with peace and love.

He gives us strength to face each day,

And guides us on His perfect way.

No longer slaves to sin and shame,

We live in Christ and praise His name.

POWER OF FORGIVENESS

The healing power of forgiveness,

Brings hope, and light, and holiness.

It cleanses us from all our sin,

And makes us new, with grace within.

It breaks the chains that bind us down,

And lifts us up, to wear a crown.

We're free in Christ, forevermore,

And live with Him, on Heaven's shore.

JOY OF REDEMPTION

The joy of redemption, so pure and so bright,

Fills our hearts with love, with peace, and with light.

It's the gift of forgiveness, so sweet and so rare,

That makes us new and fills us with care.

We're no longer slaves to sin and despair,

But free in Christ, with a heart that's fair.

We're washed by the blood that He shed on the tree,

And live forever, with Him, holy and free.

GRACE OF GOD

The grace of God, so rich and so free,

Forgives our sins and sets us free.

It's the gift of love, that Jesus gave,

To make us new and show us the way.

His mercy flows, like a gentle stream,

And washes us, to make us clean.

No longer slaves, to sin and shame,

We live in Christ and praise His name.

HOPE OF FORGIVENESS

The hope of forgiveness, so bright and so clear,

Fills our hearts with joy, with love, and with cheer.

It's the gift of God, that sets us free,

And leads us to life, eternally.

His love is boundless, His mercy deep,

He calls us close, and never sleeps.

We can trust in Him, and His grace,

For He has promised to never forsake.

UNFALLING LOVE OF GOD

The unfailing love of God, so pure and so true,

Forgives our sins and makes us new.

It's the gift of grace, that flows from above,

And fills us with peace, with joy, and with love.

His love endures, it never fades,

It lifts us up, from sin's dark shades.

No longer bound, to guilt and despair,

We live in Christ, with hearts that care.

LIVING WORD

Within the sacred pages, wisdom shines,

A living Word that breathes with life divine,

Each verse a beacon, guiding hearts and minds,

To find the truth that sets our souls alight.

Through ancient tales, the Word of God resounds,

A testament of love, and grace, and might,

In every line, the voice of hope abounds,

And leads us through the darkness to the light.

In quiet moments, let the Word unfold,

And touch your heart, your spirit, and your soul,

For in its sacred text, the truth is told,

Of love eternal, and a peace untold.

Embrace the living Word, and let it be,

A lamp unto your feet and set you free.

VOICE

Whispers in the wind,

The rustle of leaves,

The eternal voice of the Word

Echoes through the ages,

A symphony of truth,

Resounding in hearts that listen.

Boundless and timeless,

The Word of God,

A beacon of hope,

Guiding weary souls,

Through the storms of life,

To the safe harbor of grace.

Open your heart,

Let the eternal voice speak,

In the silence of your soul,

And awaken the love,

The compassion,

And the truth,

That dwells within.

LIGHT OF THE WORD

The Word of God, a light that never fades,

Illuminates the path that lies ahead,

A beacon bright, that shines through darkest shades,

And fills our hearts with hope, when all seems dead.

In times of doubt, when shadows cloud our way,

The Word stands firm, a rock on which to stand,

A refuge from the storm, a light of day,

That guides us gently to the promised land.

Embrace the light of the Word, and let it be,

A lamp unto your path, a torch ablaze,

And in its golden glow, you'll truly see,

The love and grace that fill your every day.

Hold fast the Word, and let its light consume,

The darkness in your heart, and hope resume.

WELLSPRING OF TRUTH

In the depths of the soul,

A wellspring of truth,

The Word of God,

A river that flows,

Through the landscape of our lives,

Nourishing, healing, transforming.

Drink from the waters,

And be quenched,

By the wisdom,

The love,

And the eternal promise,

That springs forth,

From the Word.

In the stillness,

Let the wellspring of truth,

Wash over your spirit,

And let the Word of God,

Flow through you,

A river of grace,

Leading you home.

THE WORDS EMBRACE

The Word of God, a love that knows no bounds,

Embraces all who seek its gentle touch,

A solace for the weary and the worn,

A refuge from the storms that rage and clutch.

In every verse, the Word's embrace is found,

A healing balm for hearts that ache and yearn,

A comfort for the lost, a guiding hand,

That leads us to the peace for which we burn.

Seek out the Word, and let its love enfold,

Your spirit, in the warmth of heaven's grace,

And in its tender arms, you'll come to know,

A love eternal, that no time can chase.

Rest in the Word's embrace, and let it be,

The anchor of your soul and set you free.

THE BREATH

In the beginning,

The breath of life,

The Word of God,

Spoke the universe into existence,

A cosmic symphony,

Of stars and galaxies,

Born from divine intention.

The same breath,

The same Word,

Resides within us,

A spark of the divine,

A reflection of the Creator,

Imbued with love,

And infinite potential.

Listen to the breath of life,

The Word that whispers,

In the depths of your being,

And let it guide you,

Through the labyrinth of life,

To the heart of truth,

Where all creation begins.

PILLARS

A pillar strong, the Word of God stands tall,

A fortress of our faith, unyielding, true,

In every trial, every tear that falls,

It holds us close and carries us anew.

When storms assail, and doubts beset our minds,

The Word remains, a shelter from the gale,

A constant source of hope, and strength combined,

To guide us through the darkness and prevail.

Hold fast the Word, and let it be the rock,

Upon which all your dreams and faith are built,

For in its sacred text, a love unlocked,

That vanquishes our fears and ends our guilt.

The pillar of our faith, the Word secure,

A foundation that will evermore endure.

ETERNITY

Silent echoes,

Resonating through time,

The Word of God,

A voice that transcends,

The boundaries of language,

And the limits of human understanding.

In the whispers of the wind,

The murmur of the river,

The song of the nightingale,

The Word speaks,

A call to the heart,

An invitation to the soul.

Embrace the echoes of eternity,

Let the Word of God,

Ring through your being,

A melody of love,

A harmony of truth,

An anthem of grace,

That will carry you home.

UNFAILING WORD

Unfailing, true, the Word of God persists,

Through countless ages, and the rise and fall,

Of empires, and the ever-changing mists,

Of time, it stands, unbroken, over all.

In times of joy, and sorrow's bitter sting,

The Word remains, a constant source of grace,

A wellspring of the love that hope will bring,

And in its tender words, our strength we trace.

Hold fast the Word, and let it be your guide,

Through every season, every change and tide,

For in its steadfast truth, we find our peace,

And in its love, a shelter that won't cease.

The Word unfailing, let it be your shield,

And in its strength, let all your fears be stilled.

THE TAPESTRY

A tapestry of truth,

Woven through the fabric of creation,

The Word of God,

A pattern of love,

A design of grace,

A masterpiece of wisdom,

That binds us all together.

In the threads of our lives,

The Word weaves,

A story of redemption,

A tale of hope,

A narrative of transformation,

That connects us to the divine.

Let the tapestry of the Word,

Enfold you in its beauty,

And let its intricate design,

Guide your steps,

Illuminate your path,

And lead you to the heart,

Of the eternal mystery.

Made in the USA
Columbia, SC
31 May 2023